D1317935

QUESTIONS
FOR THE
DALAI LAMA

QUESTIONS
FOR THE
DALAI LAMA

ANSWERS ON LOVE,
SUCCESS, HAPPINESS &
THE MEANING OF LIFE

FOREWORD BY LAUREN ALDERFER

EDITED BY DEDE CUMMINGS & TRAVIS HELLSTROM

 **hatherleigh**

Hatherleigh Press is committed to preserving and protecting the natural resources of the earth. Environmentally responsible and sustainable practices are embraced within the company's mission statement.

Visit us at www.hatherleighpress.com and register online for free offers, discounts, special events, and more.

Questions for the Dalai Lama
Text copyright © 2014 Dede Cummings and Travis Hellstrom

Library of Congress Cataloging-in-Publication Data
is available upon request.

ISBN: 978-1-57826-497-1

Cover and Interior Design by Dede Cummings
Cover photo © stevenbrock.com

Printed in the United States
10 9 8 7 6 5 4 3 2 1

CONTENTS

One of the most powerful visions I have experienced was the first photograph of the Earth from outer space. The image of a blue planet floating in deep space, glowing like the full moon on a clear night, brought home powerfully to me the recognition that we are indeed all members of a single family sharing one little house.

—His Holiness the XIV Dalai Lama

FOREWORD

NOBEL PEACE PRIZE LAUREATE, spiritual and temporal leader of the Tibetan
people, philosopher, humanitarian, promoter
of scientific understanding, simple monk—
His Holiness the XIV Dalai Lama of Tibet
represents different things to different people.
Whether addressing world leaders with the
message of peace; convening the most brilliant
minds in the scientific community to bridge
an understanding between cognitive reason
and religious practice; training thousands of
Buddhist monks while reciting ancient sutras;

shaking hands with Tibetan refugees who risked their lives crossing the Himalayas on foot in hopes of getting a glimpse of the Dalai Lama; or speaking to students at colleges in the United States; His Holiness the XIV Dalai Lama tirelessly dedicates his efforts to promote inner peace and global understanding.

It has been a profound privilege to be present in many of these settings, observing the Dalai Lama's ability to touch so many lives, including mine. Leading a typical American life in most ways, I have also had the great fortune to spend many years in India collaborating with the Tibetan community. Through these experiences, my life has forever changed; it has changed by osmosis, in large part through hearing the refrains from His Holiness the XIV Dalai Lama over many years: Do not waste this precious human life; kindness is my religion; do not harm others; love, compassion, and a sense of universal responsibility are the sources of peace and happiness.

These ideas and others included in *Questions for the Dalai Lama* gather profound thinking and deep inspiration from one of the most highly trained minds and compassionate hearts of a single individual living on the planet today. It is very heartening that this book is now widely accessible, further promoting His Holiness' message of peace and harmony to an increasingly large audience. The answers His Holiness gives are thoughts we can return to time and again: during life's challenges, when contemplating happiness, or simply when seeking an inspiration for the day. Whatever the reason may be, may their meaning seep into your heart and mind, contributing to your own inner peace and happiness; and in so do-ing, creating greater peace and happiness in the world.

—LAUREN ALDERFER

AUTHORS'
NOTE

I N E A R L Y July of 1935, The XIV Dalai Lama was born to a farming and horse-trading family in a village on the Tibetan border of China.

One of seven siblings, he was plucked from the family farm at the early age of two years old. He became the Tibetan religious and temporal ruler at 15, and then moved into exile in 1959, where he has remained until now—a spokes-man for Tibetan sovereignty and an unwaver-ing advocate for world peace.

His Holiness is the spiritual leader of the

Tibetan people, and frequently states that his life is guided by three major commitments: the promotion of basic human values, or secular ethics, in the interest of human happiness; the fostering of inter-religious harmony; and the preservation of Tibet's Buddhist culture, a tradition of peace and non-violence.

"I am just like you," he says. And indeed, the Dalai Lama *is* a humble man; he likes to tell stories and laugh at his own jokes. But his sage wisdom is meant for humankind, and it is the focus of this book.

People all over the world, regardless of their religious affiliations, respect the practical approach to living espoused by His Holiness the XIV Dalai Lama. We all relate to his charismatic way of being, which is humble, thoughtful, and giving.

For centuries, millions upon millions of people have sought out the timeless wisdom of the Dalai Lama. Tenzin Gyatso, the fourteenth and current Dalai Lama, has traveled the world and has given numerous speeches and lectures on countless humanistic topics, such as women's equality, the environment, non-violence, and human rights.

His messages resonate with everyone; it is to present these words, and to let them bolster your personal determination, that this book has been written. We have sought out His Holiness' words of wisdom, given as always, without reservation, to the people he serves. To find a list of the many books written by His Holiness and about the teachings, visit the official website of the Office of His Holiness the 14th Dalai Lama at www.dalailama.com.

"A healthy mind is the most important element for a healthy body," he told an American audience recently. "If you help others, and serve others as much as you can, that's the proper way to lead a meaningful life."

The Dalai Lama agrees that modern life has become materialistic. But still he insists: "Everything is connected, the whole world, and we must all, collectively, take action to work for peace."

It is the intention of this little book to keep the teachings of His Holiness short and accessible. Organized into five sections, *Questions for the Dalai Lama* poses universal, pertinent questions, with answers that come from the XIV Dalai Lama himself, through quotes, articles, speeches, and written works directly attributed to His Holiness.

Speaking on themes ranging from love to tragedy, success and happiness, and the crucial human skill of compassion, the following quotes have been selected to exemplify the spiritual and practical path practiced by His Holiness.

We are called as members of the human race to work together, forgetting political and national divisions; to train our minds with the discipline needed to achieve our pinnacle, and work for peace.

—FROM THE AUTHORS

We are but visitors on this planet. We are here for ninety or one hundred years at the very most. During that period, we must try to do something good, something useful with our lives. If you contribute to other people's happiness, you will find the true goal, the true meaning of life.

— HIS HOLINESS THE XIV DALAI LAMA

PART I

LOVE

Through training there is knowledge.
You can produce compassion, love,
forgiveness. You can change yourself.

—His Holiness the XIV Dalai Lama

The need for love lies at the very foundation of human existence.

—His Holiness the XIV Dalai Lama

What is the need for love?

"The reason why love and compassion bring the greatest happiness is simply that our nature cherishes them above all else. The need for love lies at the very foundation of human existence. It results from the profound interdependence we all share with one another. However capable and skillful an individual may be, left alone, he or she will not survive. However vigorous and independent one may feel during the most prosperous periods of life, when one is sick or very young or very old, one must depend on the support of others."

Without inner peace, it is impossible to have world peace. Through compassion, through love, it is possible to become a true human family. Through love we can have true happiness, real disarmament.

—HIS HOLINESS THE XIV DALAI LAMA

Is love a universal principle?

"Inter-dependence, of course, is a fundamental law of nature. Not only higher forms of life but also many of the smallest insects are social beings who, without any religion, law or education, survive by mutual cooperation based on an innate recognition of their interconnectedness. The most subtle level of material phenomena is also governed by interdependence. All phenomena from the planet we inhabit to the oceans, clouds, forests and flowers that surround us, arise in dependence upon subtle patterns of energy. Without their proper interaction, they dissolve and decay. "

Tibetan Buddhism is at one level the universal message similarly offered by Christianity—love thy neighbor as thyself. Harming or destroying any being from the highest to the lowest, from a human to the tiniest insect, must at all costs be avoided. The foundation of all spiritual practice is love.

—His Holiness the XIV Dalai Lama

How do we learn to love ourselves?

"We can never obtain peace in our outer world until we make peace with ourselves. If you do not have the capacity to love yourself, then there is simply no basis on which to build a sense of caring toward others. Human potential is the same for all. Your feeling, "I am not of value," is wrong. Absolutely wrong. You are deceiving yourself. We all have the power of thought—so what are you lacking? If you have willpower, then you can do anything.

It is usually said that you are your own master. The moment you think only of your-self, the focus of your whole mind narrows, and because of this narrow focus, uncomfortable things can appear huge and bring you fear, discomfort, and a sense of feeling over-whelmed by misery. The moment you think of others with a sense of caring, however, your mind widens. Within that wider angle, your own problems appear to be of no significance, and this makes a big difference."

The true test of honoring Buddha's or God is the love one extends to fellow humans.

—His Holiness the XIV Dalai Lama

Love and compassion are necessities, not luxuries. Without them humanity cannot survive.

—HIS HOLINESS THE XIV DALAI LAMA

Is love a natural need in humans?

"Since a child cannot survive without the care of others, love is its most important nourishment. The happiness of childhood, the allaying of the child's many fears and the healthy development of its self-confidence all depend directly upon love. Nowadays, many children grow up in unhappy homes. If they do not receive proper affection, in later life they will rarely love their parents and, not infrequently, will find it hard to love others. This is very sad.

As children grow older and enter school, their need for support must be met by their teachers. If a teacher not only imparts academic education but also assumes responsibility for preparing students for life, his or her pupils will feel trust and respect and what has been taught will leave an indelible impression on their minds. On the other hand, subjects taught by a teacher who does not show true concern for his or her students' overall well-being will be regarded as temporary and not retained for long.

If one is sick and being treated in hospital by a doctor who evinces a warm human feeling, one feels at ease and the doctor's desire to give the best possible care is itself curative, irrespective of the degree of his or her technical skill. On the other hand, if one's doctor lacks human feeling and displays an unfriendly expression, impatience, or casual disregard, one will feel anxious, even if he or she is the most highly-qualified doctor and the disease has been correctly diagnosed and the right medication prescribed. Inevitably, patients' feelings make a difference to the quality and completeness of their recovery."

You can develop the right attitude toward others if you have kindness, love, and respect for them, and a clear realization of the oneness of all human beings.

—HIS HOLINESS THE XIV DALAI LAMA

Remember that the best relationship is one in which your love for each other exceeds your need for each other.

—His Holiness the XIV Dalai Lama

Is love the desire for sex and reproduction, or something other?

"Leaving aside the complex question of the creation and evolution of our universe, we can at least agree that each of us is the product of our own parents. In general, our conception took place not just in the context of sexual desire, but from our parents' decision to have a child. Such decisions are founded on responsibility and altruism—the parents' compassionate commitment to take care of their child until it is able to take care of itself. Thus, from the very moment of our conception, our parents' love is directly in our creation."

PART II

COMPASSION

Ultimately, humanity is one and this small planet is our only home. If we are to protect this home of ours, each of us needs to experience a vivid sense of universal altruism. It is only this feeling that can remove the self-centered motives that cause people to deceive and misuse one another.

—His Holiness the XIV Dalai Lama

I believe compassion to be one of the few things we can practice that will bring immediate and long-term happiness to our lives.

—HIS HOLINESS THE XIV DALAI LAMA

What is compassion?

"First of all, we must be clear about what we mean by compassion. Many forms of compassion are mixed with desire and attachment. True compassion is not just an emotional response but also a firm commitment founded on reason. Therefore, a truly compassionate attitude toward others does not change even if they behave negatively. Through universal altruism, you develop a feeling of responsibility for others: the wish to help them actively overcome their problems.

Whether people are beautiful and friendly or unattractive and disruptive, ultimately they are human beings, just like oneself. Like oneself, they want happiness and do not want suffering. Furthermore, their right to over-come suffering and be happy is equal to one's own. Now, when you recognize that all beings are equal in both their desire for happiness and their right to obtain it, you automatically feel empathy and closeness for them. Through accustoming your mind to this sense of universal altruism, you develop a feeling of responsibility for others—the wish to help them actively overcome their problems. Nor is this wish selective; it applies equally to all. As long as they are human beings experiencing pleasure and pain just as you do, there is no logical basis to discriminate between them or to alter your concern for them if they behave negatively. Of course, developing this kind of compassion is not at all easy!"

*All major religions carry the same
messages—message of love, compassion,
forgiveness, tolerance, contentment and,
self-discipline. I have Muslim friends,
Christian friends. All have these same values.*

—HIS HOLINESS THE XIV DALAI LAMA

Buddhism has long argued for the tremendous potential for transformation that exists naturally in the human mind. To this end, the tradition has developed a wide range of contemplative techniques, or meditation practices, aimed specifically at two principal objectives: the cultivation of a compassionate heart and the cultivation of deep insights into the nature of reality, which are referred to as the union of compassion and wisdom.

— HIS HOLINESS THE XIV DALAI LAMA

What does Buddhism say about compassion?

"My religion is very simple. My religion is kindness. This is my simple religion. No need for temples. No need for complicated philosophy. Your own mind, your own heart, is the temple. Your philosophy is simple kindness."

It does not matter whether you are a theist or atheist, what matters is sincerity, forgiveness, and compassion.

—HIS HOLINESS THE XIV DALAI LAMA

How can we each make the biggest difference in the world?

"I believe that at every level of society—familial, tribal, national, and international—the key to a happier and more successful world is the growth of compassion. We do not need to become religious, nor do we need to believe in an ideology. All that is necessary is for each of us to develop our good human qualities. I try to treat whomever I meet as an old friend. This gives me a genuine feeling of happiness. It is the practice of compassion."

As human beings we all want to be happy and free from misery...we have learned that the key to happiness is inner peace. The greatest obstacles to inner peace are disturbing emotions such as anger and attachment, fear and suspicion, while love, compassion, and a sense of universal responsibility are the sources of peace and happiness.

—His Holiness the XIV Dalai Lama

If compassion is our natural state, why do we cause so much suffering?

"Some of my friends have told me that, while love and compassion are marvelous and good, they are not really very relevant. Our world, they say, is not a place where such beliefs have much influence or power. They claim that anger and hatred are so much a part of human nature that humanity will always be dominated by them. I do not agree.

We humans have existed in our present form for about a hundred thousand years. I believe that if during this time the human mind had been primarily controlled by anger and hatred, our overall population would have decreased. But today, despite all our wars, we find that the human population is greater than ever. This clearly indicates to me that love and compassion predominate in the world. And this is why unpleasant events are news, compassionate activities are so much part of daily life that they are taken for granted and, therefore, largely ignored."

If you have a sincere and open heart, you naturally feel self-worth and confidence, and there is no need to be fearful of others. If you have this basic quality of kindness or good heart, then all other things will go in the right direction.

—HIS HOLINESS THE XIV DALAI LAMA

It is our enemies who provide us with the challenge we need to develop the qualities of tolerance, patience, and compassion.

—His Holiness the XIV Dalai Lama

How do I develop compassion?

"Let me emphasize that it is within your power, given patience and time, to develop this kind of compassion. Of course, our self-centeredness, our distinctive attachment to the feeling of an independent, self-existent 'I' works fundamentally to inhibit our compassion. Indeed, true compassion can be experienced only when this type of self-grasping is eliminated. But this does not mean that we cannot start and make progress now.

We should begin by removing the greatest hindrances to compassion: anger and hatred. As we all know, these are extremely powerful emotions and they can overwhelm our entire mind. Nevertheless, they can be controlled. If, however, they are not, these negative emotions will plague us and impede our quest for the happiness of a loving mind. Compassion is by nature gentle, peaceful, and soft, but it is very powerful. It is those who easily lose their patience who are insecure and unstable. Thus, to me, the arousal of anger is a direct sign of weakness.

So, when a problem first arises, try to remain humble, maintain a sincere attitude, and be concerned that the outcome is fair. Of course, others may try to take advantage of you, and if your remaining detached only encourages unjust aggression, adopt a strong stand. This, however, should be done with compassion, and if it is necessary to express your views and take strong countermeasures, do so without anger or ill-intent."

Our prime purpose in this life is to help others. And if you can't help them, at least don't hurt them.

—His Holiness the XIV Dalai Lama

PART III

SUCCESS

*Judge your success by what you had
to give up in order to get it.*

—HIS HOLINESS THE XIV DALAI LAMA

There is no doubt about the increase in our material progress and technology, but somehow this is not sufficient, as we have not yet succeeded in bringing about peace and happiness or in overcoming suffering.

—HIS HOLINESS THE XIV DALAI LAMA

How do we achieve
success in life?

"I have found that the greatest degree of inner tranquility comes from the development of love and compassion. The more we care for the happiness of others, the greater is our own sense of well-being. Cultivating a close, warm-hearted feeling for others automatically puts the mind at ease. It is the ultimate source of success in life."

One who smiles has a happy, successful life.

—His Holiness the XIV Dalai Lama

How do we measure success in life?

"Occasionally, people who do not have a proper knowledge of karmic law say that such-and-such person is very kind and religious, but he always has problems, whereas so-and-so is very deceptive and negative, but always seems very successful. Such people may think that there is no karmic law at all. There are others who go to the other extreme and become superstitious, thinking that when someone experiences illness, it is all due to harmful spirits. However, there is a definite relation between causes and effects: that actions not committed will never produce an effect; and that once committed, actions will never lose their potentiality."

The whole purpose of religion is to fa-cilitate love and compassion, patience, tolerance, humility, and forgiveness.

—His Holiness the XIV Dalai Lama

If we are successful,
why is it so important
to help others?

"If in the midst of your enjoyment of the world you have a moment, try to help in however small a way those who are downtrodden and those who, for whatever reason, cannot or do not help themselves. Try not to turn away from those whose appearance is disturbing, from the ragged and unwell. Try never to think of them as inferior to yourself. If you can, try not even to think of yourself as better than the humblest beggar. You will look the same in your grave."

When we die, nothing can be taken with us but the seeds of our life's work and our spiritual knowledge.

—HIS HOLINESS THE XIV DALAI LAMA

Is it important to be successful in material things?

"There is no doubt about the increase in our material progress and technology, but somehow this is not sufficient, as we have not yet succeeded in bringing about peace and happiness or in overcoming suffering. If you help others with sincere motivation and sincere concern, that will bring you more fortune, more friends, more smiles, and more success. If you forget about others' rights and neglect others' welfare, ultimately you will be very lonely."

Choose to be optimistic, it feels better.

—His Holiness the XIV Dalai Lama

How do we maintain a successful and satisfying life?

"Above all, we must put others before us and keep others in our mind constantly; the self must be placed last. All our doings and thinkings must be motivated by compassion for others. The way to acquire this kind of outlook is that we must accept the simple fact that whatever we desire is also desired by others. Every being wants happiness, not suffering. If we adopt a self-centered approach to life by which we attempt to use others for our own self-interest, we might be able to gain temporary benefit, but in the long run, we will not succeed in achieving even our personal happiness, and hope for the next life is out of the question."

PART IV

LIFE'S
CHALLENGES

*I try to see each tragedy in the context
of other bigger tragedies in history. That
gives me a larger focus and makes it easier
to bear. So that is my secret, my trick.*

—His Holiness the XIV Dalai Lama

Fulfilled desire may provide a sense of temporary satisfaction; however, the pleasure we experience upon acquiring a new car or home, for example, is usually short-lived. When we indulge our desires, they tend to increase in intensity and multiply in number. We become more demanding and less content, finding it more difficult to satisfy our needs.

—HIS HOLINESS THE XIV DALAI LAMA

Why can life be so difficult?

"As long as we live in this world, we are bound to encounter problems. If, at such times, we lose hope and become discouraged, we diminish our ability to face difficulties. If, on the other hand, we remember that it is not just ourselves but also everyone who has to undergo suffering, this more realistic perspective will increase our determination and capacity to overcome troubles. Indeed, with this attitude, each new obstacle can be seen as yet another valuable opportunity to improve our mind!"

If a problem is fixable, if a situation is such that you can do something about it, then there is no need to worry. If it's not fixable, then there is no help in worrying. There is no benefit in worrying whatsoever.

—His Holiness the XIV Dalai Lama

How should we react to life's challenges?

"There is a saying in Tibetan, 'Tragedy should be utilized as a source of strength.' No matter what sort of difficulties, how painful an experience is, if we lose our hope, that's our real disaster. No matter what the circumstances, no matter what kind of tragedy I am facing, I practice compassion. This gives me inner strength and happiness. This gives me the feeling that my life is useful.

When we meet real tragedy in life, we can react in two ways: either by losing hope and falling into self-destructive habits, or by using the challenge to find our inner strength. I try to see each tragedy in the context of other bigger tragedies in history. That gives me a larger focus and makes it easier to bear. So that is my secret, my trick."

At times there have been impossible responsibilities and a lot of difficulties. Then again, personally I'm quite jovial, with not much worry. I do my best, which is moderation, and failure doesn't matter.

—HIS HOLINESS THE XIV DALAI LAMA

In the face of any real ethical challenge, we must respond in a spirit of humility, recognizing not only the limits of our knowledge (both collective and personal) but also our vulnerability to being misguided in context of such a rapidly changing reality.

—HIS HOLINESS THE XIV DALAI LAMA

What should we do first when we face a challenge?

"First we must help; then later, we can talk about the causes of any tragedy. There is an Indian saying, 'If you are struck by a poisonous arrow, it is important first to pull it out.' There is no time to ask who shot it, what sort of poison it is, and so on. First handle the immediate problem, and later investigate. Similarly, when we encounter human suffering, it is important to respond with compassion rather than to question the politics of those we help."

With care and compassion, a warm heart and determination, difficult things can change and healthy, happy people can talk through their differences, reaching a compromise that all can live with.

—His Holiness the XIV Dalai Lama

Why are people so difficult?

"Sometimes it's very difficult to explain why people do the things they do.... You'll often find that there are no simple explanations. If we were to go into the details of individual lives, since a human being's mind is so complex, it would be quite difficult to understand what is going on, what exactly is taking place. As a Buddhist monk, my concern extends to all members of the human family and, indeed, to all sentient beings who suffer. I believe all suffering is caused by ignorance. People inflict pain on others in the selfish pursuit of their happiness or satisfaction. Yet true happiness comes from a sense of brotherhood and sisterhood."

If you want to change the world, first try to improve and bring about change within yourself. That will help change your family. From there it just gets bigger and bigger. Everything we do has some effect, some impact.

—His Holiness the XIV Dalai Lama

How do I deal with difficult people?

"Merely thinking that compassion and reason and patience are good will not be enough to develop them. We must wait for difficulties to arise and then attempt to practice them. And who creates such opportunities? Not our friends, of course, but our enemies. They are the ones who give us the most trouble. So if we truly wish to learn, we should consider enemies to be our best teachers!

For a person who cherishes compassion and love, the practice of tolerance is essential, and for that, an enemy is indispensable. So we should feel grateful to our enemies, for it is they who can best help us develop a tranquil mind! Also, it is often the case in both personal and public life, that with a change in circumstances, enemies become friends. So anger and hatred are always harmful, and unless we train our minds and work to reduce their negative force, they will continue to disturb us and disrupt our attempts to develop a calm mind. Anger and hatred are our real enemies. These are the forces we most need to confront and defeat, not the temporary enemies who appear intermittently throughout life."

We need to help each other when we have difficulties, and we must share the good fortune that we enjoy.

—HIS HOLINESS THE XIV DALAI LAMA

PART V

HAPPINESS

Happiness is not something readymade.
It comes from your own actions.

—His Holiness the XIV Dalai Lama

I often believe that the basic goal or end of life is happiness, satisfaction. I believe our existence is very much based on hope.

—HIS HOLINESS THE XIV DALAI LAMA

What is the purpose of life?

"This one great question underlies our experience, whether we think about it consciously or not. I believe that the purpose of life is to be happy. From the moment of birth, every human being wants happiness and does not want suffering. Neither social conditioning nor education nor ideology affect this. From the very core of our being, we simply desire contentment. I don't know whether the universe, with its countless galaxies, stars and planets, has a deeper meaning or not, but at the very least, it is clear that we humans who live on this earth face the task of making a happy life for ourselves. Therefore, it is important to discover what will bring about the greatest degree of happiness."

Freedom is the real source of human happiness and creativity. Irrespective of whether you are a believer or nonbeliever, whether Buddhist, Christian, or Jew, the important thing is to be a good human being.

—His Holiness the XIV Dalai Lama

How do I achieve happiness?

"For a start, it is possible to divide every kind of happiness and suffering into two main categories: mental and physical. Of the two, it is the mind that exerts the greatest influence on most of us. Unless we are either gravely ill or deprived of basic necessities, our physical condition plays a secondary role in life. If the body is content, we virtually ignore it. The mind, however, registers every event, no matter how small. Hence we should devote our most serious efforts to bringing about mental peace

From my own limited experience I have found that the greatest degree of inner tranquility comes from the development of love and compassion."

There is no way that negative actions or unwholesome deeds can result in joy and happiness. Joy and happiness, by definition, are the results of fruits of wholesome actions.

—HIS HOLINESS THE XIV DALAI LAMA

What should I do, day to day, to develop happiness?

"Every day, think as you wake up, today I am fortunate to be alive, I have a precious human life, I am not going to waste it. I am going to use all my energies to develop myself, to expand my heart out to others; to achieve enlightenment for the benefit of all beings. Happiness is not something readymade. It comes from your own actions.

The basic sources of happiness are a good heart, compassion, and love. If we have these mental attitudes, even if we are surrounded by hostility, we feel little disturbance. On the other hand, if we lack compassion and our mental state is filled with anger or hatred, we will not have peace."

Though sometimes people laugh when I say it, I myself always want more friends. I love smiles. Because of this I have the problem of knowing how to make more friends and how to get more smiles, in particular, genuine smiles. If these are the smiles we want, then we ourselves must create the reasons for them to appears.

—HIS HOLINESS THE XIV DALAI LAMA

How are friendships important for happiness?

"Of course, it is natural and right that we all want friends. I often joke that if you really want to be selfish, you should be very altruistic! You should take good care of others, be concerned for their welfare, help them, serve them, make more friends, make more smiles. The result? When you yourself need help, you find plenty of helpers! If, on the other hand, you neglect the happiness of others, in the long term you will be the loser. And is friendship produced through quarrels and anger, jealousy and intense competitiveness? I do not think so. Only affection brings us genuine close friends. In today's materialistic society, if you have money and power, you seem to have many friends. But they are not friends of yours; they are the friends of your money and power. When you lose your wealth and influence, you will find it very difficult to track these people down.

The trouble is that when things in the world go well for us, we become confident that we can manage by ourselves and feel we do not need friends, but as our status and health decline, we quickly realize how wrong we were. That is the moment when we learn who is really helpful and who is completely useless. So to prepare for that moment, to make genuine friends who will help us when the need arises, we ourselves must cultivate altruism!"

Remember that sometimes not getting what you want is a wonderful stroke of luck.

—HIS HOLINESS THE XIV DALAI LAMA

From all points of view we're the same in wanting happiness and not wanting suffering. Now oneself is only one, but others are infinite in number. Therefore, others are more important than oneself.

—HIS HOLINESS THE XIV DALAI LAMA

What role do material items play in happiness?

"A very poor, underprivileged person might think that it would be wonderful to have an automobile or a television set, and should he acquire them, at the beginning he would feel very happy. Now if such happiness were something permanent, it would remain forever. But it does not; it goes. After a few months he wants to change the models. The old ones, the same objects, now cause dissatisfaction. This is the nature of change.

One of Buddhism's most relevant lessons is the avoidance of extremes. It teaches that freedom and happiness will not be found in the extremes of either sensual indulgence or mortification: a middle way must be found."

ACKNOWLEDGMENTS

W<small>E WOULD</small> like to take a moment to thank you, our readers, for being on this journey with us. We'd also like to thank our friends who volunteered to help us in writing this book, contributing questions, favorite quotes and much more. Thank you especially to Debbie Carter, Amanda Bogardus, Donna Rizzardini, Martha Black-Zapata, Paul Black, Natasha Ginnivan, and Claire Roberts.

From Travis

I would like to thank my family and friends who have encouraged me as I have researched and thought up creative ways to share the wise words of His Holiness. Thank you, Mom, for encouraging me to read *The Art of Happiness* so many years ago and Dad, Leighanna, and Elias for all the great conversations.

Thank you, Pawan, for your help and inspiration launching our Facebook page as we explored sharing His Holiness' words; Brian, for your dedication to launching our iPhone app; and Dede, of course, for making this wonderful book a reality.

Lastly I'd like to thank my wife Tunga, who continues to inspire me every day to better understand the simple but profound teachings of the Dalai Lama, simply by being the most wonderful person I've ever met.

From Dede

We could not have done this without the teachings, openness, and accessibility of His Holiness the 14th Dalai Lama. I will never forget the first time I saw the Dalai Lama, walking onto the stage at Middlebury College in the fall of 2012. He bowed to us, the audience; he was wearing the college's baseball cap (or was it the Boston Red Sox?), and the audience stood and clapped and clapped. I watched him from the reporters' box, pen in hand. I was so caught up in the emotion of seeing His Holiness on the stage, I could not write a thing. I could only cry, I was that moved; I was totally unprepared for the feelings that overcame me. I left after the talk, but the teachings and the inspiration are still a part of me, each and every day. This book is a gift—a way of giving back to His Holiness, but also to reach many readers all over the globe.

We wish to acknowledge the following people for their invaluable help in getting this book written, edited, and finally published.

First, and foremost, we would like to thank our publisher, Andrew Flach, for his unflagging support and for believing in our book. Our editorial team was superb: editor Anna Krusinski, along with support from Ryan Kennedy, and

Ryan Tumambing of Hatherleigh Press, helped us bring this book into the world.

I would like to thank my husband and children, Steve, Sam, Emma, and Joey Carmichael; my parents, Shirley Ellis Cummings and the late Robert Cummings; my dear friend and inspiration, Lauren Alderfer, along with Travis of course for stepping up to the plate and doing amazing work to foster the teachings of the Dalai Lama.

Last, but not least, I'd like to thank Marit Cranmer, Steven Rockefeller, John Elder, Steven Brock, Middlebury College, Vermont Public Radio, Sonam Zoksang, Dr. Tara Doyle, Rajiv Mehrotra, and the wonderful poeple who work with His Holiness; and most of all, I wish to thank His Holiness the XIV Dalai Lama, for bring his teachings and philosophy out into the world, and helping the people of Tibet reclaim their soverignity.

We'd love to hear from you and have your help developing future questions for the Dalai Lama. Share your thoughts and favorite quotes with us at questions.advancehumanity.com.

RESOURCES

Advance Humanity

This book was inspired in part by the work of Advance Humanity, a community of everyday humanitarians who are changing the world together. Founded by author Travis Hellstrom, Advance Humanity empowers people to be the change they wish to see in the world. To learn more, visit www.advancehumanity.com.

Mobile App: Dalai Lama quotes

A free iPhone and iPad app developed in partnership between Advance Humanity and

Reason Interactive, *Dalai Quotes* is a collection of hundreds of quotes from His Holiness the Dalai Lama and is the highest rated Dalai Lama app currently available in the App Store. Download it for free at www.dalaiquotes.com.

FACEBOOK: DALAI LAMA QUOTES
Social media can be an overwhelming space online. We've created a special Facebook page that features two new quotes from His Holiness the Dalai Lama everyday so that you can fill your News Feed with inspiring and supportive words. Visit www.facebook.com/quotesdalailama to follow along.

OFFICIAL WEBSITE
The official website of the Office of His Holiness the 14th Dalai Lama is a great resource. Explore here how His Holiness fulfils these commitments through his various activities his public talks, widespread international visits and publications. Visit www.dalailama.com.

AFTERWORD

T HE SPIRITUAL leader of the Tibetan people, a Nobel Peace Prize laureate, and a voice of peace and reason in our troubled time, His Holiness the 14th Dalai Lama was recently quoted as saying that the 21st century should be a century of dialogue. "There will certainly be more problems," he said, "in the years to come, but they should be dealt with through respect and compromises, not violence. Only this can serve the long-term benefits of mankind."

It is our hope, as editors of this simple, open-hearted, and luminous volume, that the reader will be inspired, enriched, and enlightened by the teachings within. When we ask, "What is mindfulness?" we will know that it is a question that does not need to be asked.

His Holiness' messages resonate with everyone; it is to present these words, and to let them bolster your personal determination, that this book has been written. We have sought out His Holiness' words of wisdom, given as always, without reservation, to the people he serves.

To find a list of the many books written by His Holiness and about the teachings, visit the official website of the Office of His Holiness the 14th Dalai Lama at www.dalailama.com.

Be kind whenever possible. It is always possible.

—His Holiness the XIV Dalai Lama

5.13
To cover all the earth with sheets of leather—
Where could such amounts of skin be found?
But with the leather soles of just my shoes
It is as though I cover all the earth!

—SHANTIDEVA,
The Way of the Bodhisattva

A NOTE ON THE DALAI LAMA TRUST

THE DALAI Lama Trust was founded in 2009 by His Holiness the 14th Dalai Lama. The trust was established to support the advancement and welfare of the Tibetan people, the culture and heritage of the ancient civilization of Tibet, and the promotion of the deep-rooted values associated with its culture and people.

Among a number of charitable activities,

the Dalai Lama Trust supports the preservation of Tibetan culture and the development of leadership and educational opportunities for young Tibetans. The trust also seeks to support initiatives that encourage a sense of universal responsibility in the global community, and the advancement of dialogue between science and religion. The trust regards the cultivation of *ahimsa* and nonviolence as a powerful means toward both individual growth and broader social change. The trust also provides relief and assistance to underserved communities of all faiths and origins.

The Dalai Lama Trust is funded by charitable contributions made by the founder and by the public. The trust is a U.S. nonprofit charitable organization registered in the State of New York. It is governed by a board of trustees, chaired by the founder.

For more information, visit www.dalailama-trust.org.